THE
SECOND
GENERATION

Church Leaders After the Apostles

By James Byers

The Second Generation: Church Leaders After the Apostles

ISBN 978-1-7342711-7-1

Written by James Byers
Cover Design by Whitnee Clinard
Book Block Design by Whitnee Clinard
Edited by Marie Byers, Rosemary J. Hilliard, Kevin Jones, and Jessa R. Sexton

Published by
Hilliard Press
a division of
The Hilliard Institute for Educational Wellness

Franklin, Tennessee
Oxford, England
Abbeyleix, Ireland

www.hilliardinstitute.com

TABLE

OF

CONTENTS

INTRODUCTION

This work addresses the progress of Christianity after the initial founding of the church. I express deep appreciation to my wife, Marie, for her assistance in the writing and editing of the book. My hope is to give a correct analysis of the lasting influence of the early leaders who would affect future generations of believers.

James Byers

THE
SECOND
GENERATION

Church Leaders After the Apostles

The apostles of Jesus are mentioned at various times in the New Testament, but only a few receive great attention. Peter, James, and John are mentioned often in the gospel writings. Paul is the center of attention in his own writings and in the Book of Acts. Family life of these men is mostly absent in the record. Peter is married, and Paul adds that some of the apostles were also married. John, the Apostle, speaks of children in his letters, but these children are not specified by name.

However, later in his life, Peter refers to John Mark as his "son in Christ" (1 Peter 5:13 ERV). Paul refers to Timothy as "my dear son" (2 Timothy 1:2 NIV) and Titus as "a true son to me in the faith we share together" (Titus 1:4 ERV). These passages demonstrate that both Peter and Paul adopted spiritual sons in their ministries.

To share some insight into why they were mentioned in this way and explain why they're deemed second generation leaders of the church, John Mark, Timothy, and Titus will be examined in this study.

Please note that family life is often not as detailed in the New Testament as in the Old Testament, but every effort has been made to avoid speculation.

JOHN MARK

John Mark introduces himself in his gospel in this way: "one of those following Jesus was a young man wearing only a linen cloth" (Mark 14:51 ERV).

Mark lived at home, probably in the vicinity of the Garden of Gethsemane. The great commotion on the night of the betrayal of Jesus Christ would have aroused John Mark from his sleep. When he approached the scene, he was grabbed and escaped wearing only underclothes, as explained in the verse above.

For Mark this was a time of trauma and a dramatic introduction to Jesus. The safety of his home proved to be a place of refuge. Why Mark refused to identify himself in the verse gave credence to the fact that he was both an eyewitness to the terrible scene and embarrassed that he fled for his own safety.

The scriptures tell us more about this scene:

> While Jesus was still speaking, Judas, one of the twelve apostles, came there. He had a big crowd of people with him, all carrying swords and clubs. They had been sent from the leading priests, the teachers of the law, and the older Jewish leaders. Judas planned to do something to show them which one was Jesus. He said, "The one I kiss will be Jesus. Arrest him and guard him while you lead him away." So Judas went over to Jesus and said, "Teacher!" Then he kissed him. The men grabbed Jesus and arrested Him. One of the followers standing near Jesus grabbed his sword and pulled it out. He swung it at the servant of the high priest and cut off his ear. Then Jesus said, "You come to get me with swords and clubs as if I were a criminal? Every day I was with you teaching in the temple area. You did not arrest me there. But all these things have happened to show the full meaning of what the Scriptures said." Then all of Jesus' followers left him and ran away. (Mark 14:43–50 ERV)

In the Book of Acts, we are introduced to John Mark because Peter goes to the house of John Mark's mother after Peter's miraculous release from prison. This story is told in the twelfth chapter of Acts of the Apostles. The story has elements of faith and occasional humor.

Peter has been placed in prison in Jerusalem. James, an apostle and brother of John, had already been executed by King Herod. Peter was about to experience a similar fate. At night he was sleeping soundly when an angel woke him from sleep. Peter was then led to the city gate of Jerusalem. The gate opened and Peter was left alone by the angel. Peter then realized this was real and not a dream.

After some pondering of his circumstances, he went to the home of Mary who was described as the mother of John Mark. A servant girl reluctantly let him into the home. Peter then told the assembled crowd about his release. James, the brother of Jesus, was not at this gathering. Peter instructed this house church to inform James of his release.

Scholar R. B. Rackham comments on this scene:

> This introduces us to another Mary, another one of those women whose praise was in the early church. The gate, the gateway into the courtyard, and the maid or portress, indicate the residence of a well-to-do family. The house being spacious had become a kind of centre in the church. Mary was a widow, and of note in the church. She was related to Barnabas. Peter calls her son John, my son. His voice is well known to the portress, and when released from prison, it is to Mary's house that he turns his steps.[1]

The story would indicate that John Mark was in this church home and that Peter was familiar with him. Peter calling Mark his son would mean that a strong bond had been made. From his youth, Mark became a believer and was familiar with the most influential disciples of the Jerusalem church.

The location of his mother's home would mean that Mark was close to many activities. The scene at Gethsemane would be close to home and would explain his comments about the unidentified person at the betrayal. Rackham comments on Peter's appearance at Mary's house, "And when, for fear of attracting notice, he had secured silence by beckoning with his hand, he told them what had happened, almost we imagine in the words which we now read, and which was drunk in by the eager ears of John Mark."[2]

The church expanded in Jerusalem, and by the 15th chapter of Acts, a conference was called to discuss future logistics concerning the gospel message. In this conference there is a composition of the old and new. The established Jewish element was represented by Peter and James, the brother of Jesus. The newer group of Christians was represented by Paul of Tarsus who had a zeal for missionary work. Paul was joined by Barnabas, a believer from Cyprus, who was related to John Mark. This conference became a defining event for the future of Christianity.

Before this Jerusalem conference, Acts 13 documents a mission effort beyond the area of Judea. The focus is on the church in the city of Antioch. Several leading church members are listed in this chapter including Barnabas, Symeon, Lucius, Manaen, and Saul. This chapter notes that the Holy Spirit revealed the plan for expansion, including the selection of Barnabas and Saul (later called Paul). The church fasted and prayed and laid hands on these two and endorsed the mission effort.

Their first stop on the journey was Seleucia, the port city of Antioch. From this port they sailed to Cyprus. This was a logical destination, for Barnabas had a home there. On Cyprus they went to the city of Salamis and proclaimed the gospel in the synagogue. John Mark is introduced at this point and is called an *attendant*. The Greek word used for *attendant* is *huperetes*, which can mean a servant.[3] The word is specifically used for attendants in synagogues.

John Mark helped Paul and Barnabas in a variety of ways. It's speculated that John Mark kept a journal and helped find contacts for their ministry. Barnabas likely knew some of the more important citizens of Cyprus. He was a landowner, and his contacts could include government officials.

While on this island, the missionaries would baptize their converts. Rackham explains:

> It is not unlikely that the apostles required personal service. But we have observed that that is not the custom of the apostles—neither Peter nor Paul—to baptize with their own hands. So baptism might be a service for the attendant. And we notice that John is mentioned in connection with the preaching in the synagogues, on which we might expect some baptisms to follow.[4]

When the missionaries reached Paphos, a major city of the island, they encountered a sorcerer-magician whose name is translated as *Elymas*. He soon attempted to exploit the teachings of Paul and Barnabas. The missionaries also encountered a man by the name of Sergius Paulus, who was titled as proconsul of Cyprus. The proconsul conducted a favorable hearing with the missionaries, and Elymas was blinded by the power of a miracle for attempting to exploit the gospel.

John Mark thus observed the power of God through these two missionaries, and he observed the great conversion which took place in Cyprus. Rackham concluded:

> The real importance of the incident, however, does not turn upon the question of an individual conversion. It is the first appearance of Christianity before the Roman aristocracy and authorities, and so it is the first step in the new stage of the progress

of the gospel, which will lead on to the appearance of Paul before the emperor himself. And when Christianity does appear before the Roman world it is with dramatic effect, with a striking conviction of false religion.[5]

The effect upon the apostles must have been no less. They also were astonished. The success of their first utterance in a court of a procounsel must have enlarged their hope and broadened their horizon.

Paul was a Roman citizen with a privilege that he had not fully valued. He had a call to stand in witness before the Gentiles, and the conversion of Sergius Paulus fired his expectation of converting the Roman Empire. His goal would be to go to Rome.[6] This would be in the future, but a change in goal for the apostles would date from this time.

This was clarified by a change in the name of Saul to Paul. In the court of Sergius Paulus, the apostle had stood as a Roman citizen. From now on his work would be in the Roman world. He would travel as a Roman and as a citizen of the empire. Paul's sudden vigor brings him to the front of the mission team.[7] The story began with Barnabas and Saul, and it became Paul and his company. The incident in Paphos, including the blinding of Elymas, a false magician, demonstrated that Paul possessed great power, and that the hand of the Lord was with him.[8]

The reaction of the mission work in Cyprus was not recorded in the Book of Acts. Mark was recorded as an attendant and a witness to the works of Paul. As mentioned earlier of the duties of being attendant, Mark would be involved with baptisms. He might have kept a journal which would prove the events such as the encounter on the island of Cyprus. In Acts 13:13 (ERV) the writer Luke recorded, "Paul and the people with him sailed away from Paphos. They came to Perga, a city of Pamphilia. There John Mark left them and returned to Jerusalem." This verse has caused a great deal of speculation. There could be no doubt that some problem existed.

Reasons for Mark's departure have been many. As he was a young man and by himself, was the journey challenging? Barnabas, his cousin, did not prevent the departure. But the city of Perga had not proven a difficulty for Mark.

In the mix, the writer of Acts would later disclose that the departure displeased Paul. This account also recorded the disagreement of Paul with Barnabas.

The various theories as to Mark's departure include that Mark was heading to a new country, a distance farther from Jerusalem, to an easier place to minister. Rackham excludes this theory. But Asia Minor was by no means a *terra incognito*, full of terror to the Jews, and John Mark was prepared for mission work. Further, if it had been a case of simple cowardice, it is not likely that Luke would have recorded it. The case would have been otherwise if it had been a matter of policy. Now it is significant that he returned to Jerusalem, and that here, and in verse five, he is still called by his Hebrew name of John and not as Mark.

Paul looked upon this departure as apostasy and not going to the work, and that would account for his severity towards Mark. It became not a personal matter but a matter of principle. As Rackham concludes, "John Mark was unable to keep pace with the rapid expansion of Paul's views of the work in the Gentile world."[9]

The scholar F. F. Bruce has a different explanation for Mark's return to Jerusalem: "We are not told the reason for his return. It may have been because of the abandonment of the original itinerary, or because he resented his cousin's falling into the second place, or some other cause we do not know."[10] Bruce writes:

> From Paphos the missionaries took ship again and sailed to Perga, a port of the south coast of Asia Minor. If Cyprus were dear to the heart of Barnabas, Asia Minor for a similar reason was dear to Paul's. And in Asia Minor it is Paul who seems to take the lead. It may have been for this reason that John Mark left them at this point and went home to Jerusalem. Possibly he had not bargained for the extension of their tour and did not like the way his cousin Barnabas seemed to be slipping into the second place. Paul, at any rate, thought there was no justification for Mark's departure and considered that he had let them down.[11]

During the conference in Jerusalem, Mark (in all probability) was there. Testimony was given by Paul and Barnabas as to their missionary journey. Acts 15 records the encouragement of the Antioch church to visit Jerusalem:

> So the group decided to send Paul, Barnabas, and some others to Jerusalem to talk more about this with the apostles and elders. [The topic was the salvation of non-Jewish believers.] The church helped them get ready to leave on their trip. The men went through the countries of Phoenicia and Samaria, where they told all about how the non-Jewish people had turned to the true God. This made all the believers very happy. When the men arrived in Jerusalem, the apostles, the elders, and the whole church welcomed them. Paul, Barnabas, and the

others told all that God had done with them. (Acts 15:2–4 ERV)

This is an effective summary of the first missionary journey, which must have been a long story if all details were given. If Mark was at this conference, he knew about the success which occurred in Cyprus. Speculation could be made that he was fully informed about the success in Asia Minor.

Mark had not been present when Paul delivered his sermon at Antioch Pisidia in the synagogue. This sermon recalled God leading the people of Israel to the land of Canaan. In Acts 13, Paul emphasized that the rescue had elevated Israel: "And during the time our people lived in Egypt as foreigners, he made them great. Then he brought them out of that country with great power. And he was patient with them for 40 years in the desert. God destroyed seven nations in the land of Canaan and gave their land to his people" (Acts 13:17-19 ERV).

Paul then continued Jewish history including the rise of the Jewish monarchy. Paul mentioned that David the king was a direct ancestor of Jesus. He then mentioned John the Baptist as a predictor of the coming of Jesus. Paul also told his audience of the crucifixion and the resurrection of Jesus Christ.

The sermon proved to be a success, and the audience invited Paul and Barnabas to return the next Sabbath. The Book of Acts records, "After the meeting, many of the people followed Paul and Barnabas, including many Jews and people who had changed their religion to worship the true God like Jews. Paul and Barnabas encouraged them to continue trusting in God's grace" (Acts 13:43 ERV).

Paul and Barnabas remembered that they were forced to leave and go to another city called Iconium. While in Iconium and preaching in the synagogue, they managed to divide the city: "They spoke to the people there. They spoke so well that many Jews and Greeks believed what they said. But some of the Jews did not believe. They said things that caused the non-Jewish people to be angry and turn against the Lord's followers" (Acts 14:1–2 ERV).

Some of the opposition planned to harm Paul and Barnabas, so they moved to a city called Lystra and later to a city called Derbe. In Lystra, Paul performed a miracle that caused a lame man to walk. The people believed that Paul and Barnabas were Greek gods and identified them as Zeus and Hermes. Both Paul and Barnabas quenched the zealous fire of these people and stated that they were but mortals and messengers of Good News. In the city of Lystra their visit ended abruptly when a mob from Antioch and Iconium stoned Paul but were unsuccessful in killing him.

These missionaries then returned to Derbe and previous cities where they chose elders for each church. With their mission trip completed, they returned to the seaport of Attalia near Perga. The sea voyage returned them to Antioch of Syria. They then went to Jerusalem. As Bruce mentions:

> As for Paul, others might undertake that part of the servant's vocation which had to do with Israel; he knew himself called to fulfill that part of it which involved the carrying of God's saving light among the Gentiles, near and far. Many others were engaged in Gentile evangelization but none with the overall strategic planning conceived in Paul's mind and so largely executed by his dynamic energy. This energy was the fruit of his conviction that he was a figure of eschatological significance, a key agent in the progress of salvation history, a chosen instrument in the Lord's hands to bring Gentiles

into the obedience of faith as a necessary prepara-
tion for the ultimate salvation of all Israel and the
consummation of God's redeeming purpose for
the world.[12]

John Mark must have wondered about the testimony of Paul.
If he were present at the Jerusalem conference, he must have
realized that his trip to Cyprus was only the beginning of a vast
mission effort in the Gentile world. While at the conference, he
would have also heard the testimony of his other mentor, the
Apostle Peter. The fifteenth chapter of Acts revealed Peter's testimony at the conference:

> After a long debate, Peter stood up and said to them,
> "My brothers, I am sure you remember what hap-
> pened in the early days. God chose me from among
> you to tell the Good News to those who are not
> Jewish. It was from me that they heard the Good
> News and believed. God knows everyone, even
> their thoughts and he accepted these non-Jewish
> people. He showed this to us by giving them the
> Holy Spirit the same as he did to us. When they
> believed, God made their hearts pure. So now, why
> are you putting a heavy burden around the necks of
> the non-Jewish followers? Are you trying to make
> God angry? We and our fathers were not able to
> carry that burden. No, we believe that we and these
> people will be saved the same way—by grace of the
> Lord Jesus." (Acts 15:7-13 ERV)

Perhaps Mark recalled the story of Peter's visit to Cornelius in
the city of Caesarea and his message to the household. Peter

had spoken to Cornelius and his relatives and servants. He told Cornelius:

> I now realize how true it is that God does not show favoritism but accepts from every nation the one who fears him and does what is right. You know the message God sent to the people of Israel, announcing the good news of peace through Jesus Christ, who is Lord of all. You know what has happened throughout the province of Judea, beginning in Galilee after the baptism that John preached—how God anointed Jesus of Nazareth with the Holy Spirit and power, and how he went around doing good and healing all who were under the power of the devil, because God was with him. We are witnesses of everything he did in the country of the Jews and in Jerusalem. They killed him by hanging him on a cross, but God raised him from the dead on the third day and caused him to be seen. He was not seen by all the people, but by witnesses whom God had already chosen—by us who ate and drank with him after he rose from the dead. He commanded us to preach to the people and to testify that he is the one whom God appointed as judge of the living and the dead. All the prophets testify about him that everyone who believes in him receives forgiveness of sins through his name. (Acts 10:34–43 NIV)

Probably Mark had heard this story. And whether he was at the Jerusalem conference or not, he would have been aware of Peter's account. The decision of James, the brother of Jesus, to "not make things hard for those who have turned to God from among the non-Jews" (Acts 15:19 ERV) must have resonated with Mark.

He is ready to again do mission work where ever the journey prescribed. And the second missionary effort is ready to begin.

Paul and Barnabas then left Jerusalem and returned to Antioch, confident that messianic work could be done. Antioch had become a special place for both Paul and Barnabas. It was Barnabas who had brought Paul to Antioch. Acts 11:19–26 (ASV) reminds us of those joyful days:

> They therefore that were scattered abroad upon the tribulation that arose about Stephen traveled as far as Phoenicia, and Cyprus, and Antioch, speaking the word to none save only to Jews. But there were some of them, men of Cyprus and Cyrene, who, when they were come to Antioch, spake unto the Greeks also, preaching the Lord Jesus. And the hand of the Lord was with them: and a great number that believed turned unto the Lord. And the report concerning them came to the ears of the church which was in Jerusalem: and they sent forth Barnabas as far as Antioch: who, when he was come, and had seen the grace of God, was glad; and he exhorted them all, that with purpose of heart they would cleave unto the Lord: for he was a good man, and full of the Holy Spirit and of faith: and much people were added unto the Lord. And he went forth to Tarsus to seek for Saul; and when he had found him, he brought him unto Antioch. And it came to pass, that even for a whole year they were gathered together with the church, and taught much people; and that the disciples were called Christians first in Antioch.

The Antioch church was to bless the work of Paul and Barnabas. As Rackham points out, "For this church was to become the great

Hellenist or Greek church, holding a position half-way between the Hebrew church of Jerusalem and the Gentile church founded by S Paul."[13]

After the conference in Jerusalem and a return to Antioch, Paul scolded both Peter, who was visiting this great city, and Barnabas for their neglect of the Gentile Christians. After these encounters, Paul, perhaps to mend the hurt feelings, urged Barnabas to join him in visiting the churches of the first missionary trip. Barnabas wanted to bring his relative John Mark, but Paul refused to accept Mark as a partner. As Bruce comments:

> But when they were on the point of setting out, Barnabas proposed that they should take Mark with them, as they had done on the earlier occasion. Paul refused point-blank; he had not forgotten Mark's desertion in the course of the previous tour. Neither Barnabas nor Paul would give way, and the upshot was that instead of one missionary expedition from Antioch this time there were two. For Barnabas and Mark went to Cyprus, while Paul went to Asia Minor.[14]

As Rackham further observes:

> Paul, however, had not forgotten Mark's desertion of them at Perga, for so it seemed to him still, and to take him with them was not right. Perhaps in the recent discussions in Antioch, Mark had been persuaded for the Hebrew point of view. Thus, a sharp contention arose between Paul and Barnabas. These two great leaders separated and never worked together again. Barnabas disappeared from

the history of Acts. Sadness occurred and the more so when we remember that Paul was introduced to the church and later his missionary work by Barnabas. Paul must have regretted the separation as he remembered he suffered greatly because of their separation even of friendship. In Philippians 3:7-8 thankfully the friendship was amended, and Paul wrote to the Corinthians that he and Barnabas were of the same mind. At the last, even Mark had won the confidence of Paul. The increase was for good works. Two missionary parties started now instead of one, and two sets of workers were taken into the field.[15]

The story of Mark disappears from the account in Acts. Speculation can be made as to what happened to Mark in the coming years. Certainly, there could be a return to Cyprus with Barnabas. But Mark was also active in Judea. As Peter spoke of him as his "son in Christ" (1 Peter 5:13) both worked together for a period.

Peter wrote his letters to Turkey, then Asia Minor provinces. Mark was in all probability there. Peter had been familiar with Mark's home in Jerusalem, and Mark was probably quite involved with the work there. Reconciliation with Paul would later become a major factor in Mark's life.

God is the author of reconciliation through His grace. It is left for humanity to accept this grace that comes through Jesus Christ. In the case of Mark, first readings of the text indicate that Mark abandoned his duty towards Paul and the message of God. However, Barnabas seemed to defend his cousin as having legitimate reasons for leaving the work.

There is no clear answer to the puzzle as to why Mark went back to Jerusalem. However, Mark suddenly reappeared when Paul sent a letter to the Colossian church. In Colossians 4:10 Paul wrote, "You have received instructions about him; if he comes to you, welcome him" (NIV). This directive by Paul implies that a reconciliation had taken place. Biblica, the International Bible Society, observed, "At this point Mark was apparently beginning to win his way back into Paul's confidence . . . By the end of Paul's life, Mark had fully regained Paul's favor."[16]

The confidence that Paul had in sending Mark as an emissary to the Colossians with Paul's instructions seemed to be more than just a slight confidence. John Mark obviously became one of the brighter lights of the gospel message in enthusiasm and knowledge.

The story of Paul's letter to the Colossians exposed troubling problems concerning the nature of Christ. Jesus Christ was deemed insufficient to the needs of the Colossian brethren who had been introduced to the so-called Gnostic heresy. Gnostic teachers had persuaded Christians that God was to be approached in several ways. Paul was attempting to persuade these Colossians that Jesus was the Way, and He would meet their needs. Intermediary beings and esoteric rituals were not necessary, neither were certain rituals that had become part of the heresy. Mark must have become aware of the problems of this church and had been chosen by Paul to convey pertinent messages introduced and sanctioned by Paul.

Later Paul mentioned Mark in a letter to Timothy. In his last letter to Timothy, Paul wrote, "Get Mark and bring him with you when you come. He can help me in my work here" (2 Timothy 4:11 ERV). This passage is most comforting as it shows the reconciliation of the two. Also noticeable is the friendship of Timothy and Mark.

The passage also indicates that Mark had a special talent that proved helpful to Paul. Paul still believed that he had work to do, and one could certainly speculate that Mark (who had certain gifts, including writing) would be of great help. Mark obviously became a close Christian friend to both Peter and Paul. They saw in Mark the tremendous promise of the next generation.

The Book of Mark is considered by many scholars as the first of the gospels. The Gospel of Mark could have been written as early as the 50s. The church fathers associate the gospel with Peter and with the city of Rome. The gospel also points to a Jewish background, thus explaining the gospel message to Jew and Gentile alike.

In Eusebius's *Church History*, chapter 111, Papias, who was a bishop in the city of Hieropolis near Colossae, comments:

> Mark who became Peter's interpreter, wrote accurately, though not in order all that he remembered of the things said and done by the Lord. For he had neither heard the Lord nor been one of his followers, but afterwards as I said, he had followed Peter, who used to compose his discourses with a view to the needs of his hearers, but not as if he were composing a systematic account of the Lord's sayings. So Mark did nothing blameworthy, thus writing some things just as he remembered them, for he was careful of this one thing to omit none of the things he had heard and to make no untrue statement therein.[17]

Mark did not begin his gospel with a genealogy. As he did not make any allusion to the destruction of Jerusalem, he probably wrote the gospel around 50–60 A.D. He was probably in his 20s when Jesus was crucified, and he may have heard Jesus teach in Judea. In more likelihood he was familiar with John the Baptist. His gospel begins with the arrival and teaching of John in the wilderness. John would have influenced many with his bold preaching. Since we connect Mark with his mother Mary, it is possible they both heard the Spirit's message.

Mark wrote his gospel in a concise, action-filled style. He immediately referred to the baptism of Jesus by John. The ministry of Jesus then follows with rapid summaries of His selection of disciples and His performance of miracles. The healing of the demon-possessed man in Capernaum is of particular interest. Jesus had amazed His hearers, and when He healed the man, the crowd was even more amazed. Mark 1:27-28 (ERV) records the event:

> The people were amazed. They asked each other, "What is happening here? This man is teaching something new, and he teaches with authority! He even commands evil spirits, and they obey him." So the news about Jesus spread quickly everywhere in the area of Galilee.

Mark followed with a series of healings including Simon Peter's mother-in-law, a leper, and a crippled man. The people were amazed. "Immediately the paralyzed man stood up. He picked up his mat and walked out of the room. Everyone could see him. They were amazed and praised God. They said, 'This is the most amazing thing that we have ever seen'" (Mark 2:12 ERV).

Mark then turned to the battle Jesus had with Judaic legalism. His choosing Matthew as a disciple and subsequent fellowship with the tax collectors and other outcasts, His followers picking up grain stalks on the Sabbath, and finally His healing a crippled man on the Sabbath day completed the conflict. Although each incident was different, Mark showed that they all emphasize the joy of good works that Jesus was very interested in, beyond strict observance of ceremonial laws. Mark reinforced his personality of action, and he reminded his readers of the need to overcome a ceremony that hinders relationship with God.

Quickly Mark finished Jesus' selection of disciples and in his fourth chapter presented an extended parable. The parable of the productive seed would appeal to both Jew and Gentile. The chapter ends with the calming of the waters on the Sea of Galilee as Jesus crossed the sea. Burton Coffman in his commentary writes:

> Mark's purpose in his gospel shines in such as this, of which there are a number of examples. He intended that the mighty works of Christ should lead to the identification of Jesus Christ as a supernatural person, one with the Father, and fully able to give eternal life to them that come into God through him.[18]

Mark gave a very detailed history of the final days of John the Baptist in chapter six of his gospel. Mark's account of the entire story includes the feast given in the home of Herod Antipas. Coffman further indicates that Mark's account was "about twice as many words but adds no more information than Luke."[19] The supposition or speculation could be that Mark had actual contact with the Baptist, and this story was known to him in all its details. The speculation is really a moot point as the death of John was a real tragedy to the gospel writers.

Mark also recorded the clash between ceremonial law defilement and that of actual defilement. One of the examples in chapter seven explores the washing of hands. Coffman plainly refutes the ceremonial worship when he writes, "As clearly as Christ could have stated it, the principle is laid out here that the worship of God which consists in the observance of human traditions and precepts is useless. Thus, the question of overwhelming importance regarding the worship of God must be the question of authority."[20]

Later on in this chapter Mark gave an example of Jesus reaching out beyond Israel. This would appeal to Gentile readers. The example is the casting out of a demon in a woman's house in Phoenicia. The demon had possessed the woman's daughter. The miracle emphasizes that Jesus is now teaching the Gentile world.

Mark emphasized that Jesus is the Christ through the great confession of Peter at Caesarea Philippi. In Mark's gospel the confession is more succinct than the same confession recorded in the Gospel of Matthew. Coffman conjectures, "This is a much briefer account of Peter's confession than is found in Matthew, indicating perhaps that Peter, who was Mark's mentor, had not stressed the confession as strongly as the other apostles would remember, thus probably due to consideration of modesty on Peter's part."[21]

Coffman further comments that this confession is a watershed in Mark's gospel:

> To the point, the great thrust of the gospel was directed to establishment of our Lord as a divine person reaching its glorious climax in Peter's confession of the Christ. The second half of the gospel is the road to Calvary marked here at the outset with the first confession of his Passion and a dramatic shift of the Master's teaching to the phase of personal instruction for the apostles and away from the teaching the multitudes.[22]

Mark featured the transfiguration as a pivotal scene for the disciples of Jesus. Jesus had asserted His purpose, and the disciples had been slow to comprehend. Earle McMillan observes that while Jesus' awareness of his life and surroundings on earth paralleled that of other human beings—Jesus' difference lay in His incarnate nature in a human body.[23]

From chapter 11 of Mark through the end of Mark's gospel, Jesus proceeded towards the end of His earthly mission. McMillian records, "There is a certain act of finality present." When Jesus cleanses the Temple, McMillan notes that "Jesus could be aggressive, exacting and even forceful.[24]

Jesus mentioned His purpose in the anointing at Bethany in chapter 14. An unnamed woman anointed Jesus, pouring an expensive perfume over His head. As McMillan adds:

> This woman's act should probably be regarded as a classic sermon in silence, for Jesus commented, what she has done will be told in memory of her. The woman said nothing, but in her action had preached one of the most meaningful and articulate of sermons. The incident then became one of the most dramatic examples of the interpretation of any event in Mark's gospel. In this unique story a tremendous gift in terms of love and sacrifice was expressed. Jesus defended the woman's supposed extravagance because he recognized the depth of what she had done.[25]

Further statements in Mark's gospel seem to indicate a close reliance on the association of Peter and Mark. As McMillan observes the importance of Jesus being the Anointed One of God in Mark's gospel and that Peter's preaching was concerned with this as well. Mark's writing about Christ's confrontations with demonic powers emphasizes the amazement that Mark found in the life of Jesus. Mark emphasized the silence of Jesus when wonders and miracles were performed. Again, McMillan notes:

> Whatever the nature of the situation, individual or collective, the question of the Messianic Secret must remain something of an enigma. If, however, one sees the role of the demons and the ultimate triumph of Jesus over the forces of Satan as of particular importance, one is compelled to observe that the central issue in both cases was whether or not Jesus was the son of God.[26]

Mark's gospel can be summarized as a vivid account of Jesus using such words as *immediately, fear,* and *amazement.* The gospel ends with the women who went to the tomb where Jesus had been placed:

> And entering the tomb, they saw a young man sitting at the right, wearing a white robe; and they were amazed. But he said to them, "Do not be amazed; you are looking for Jesus the Nazarene, who has been crucified. He has risen; He is not here; see here is the place where they laid Him. But go, tell His disciples and Peter, "He is going ahead of you to Galilee; there you will see Him, just as he told you." And they went out and fled from the tomb; for trembling and astonishment had gripped them; and they said nothing to anyone, for they were afraid. (Mark 16:5–7 NASB)

One of the last important elements to note about Mark comes from looking at a letter Paul wrote to Philemon. Paul closed his words with "Epaphras is a prisoner with me for Christ Jesus. He sends you his greetings. Also, Mark, Aristarchus, Demas, and Luke send their greetings. They are workers together with me" (Philemon 1:23–24 ERV). Mark thus joined the coterie of companions with whom Paul worked while he was in prison.

TIMOTHY

The story of Paul's introduction to Timothy is told by Luke in Acts chapter 16:

> Paul went to the city of Derbe and then to Lystra, where a follower of Jesus named Timothy lived. Timothy's mother was a Jewish believer, but his father was a Greek. The believers in the cities of Lystra and Iconium had only good things to say about him. Paul wanted Timothy to travel with him, but all the Jews living in that area knew that his father was a Greek. So Paul circumcised Timothy to please the Jews. (Acts 16:1–3 ERV)

The closeness of Paul to Timothy is revealed in Paul's letters. In 2 Timothy Paul wrote, "To Timothy, a dear son to me. Grace, mercy, and peace to you from God the Father and from Christ Jesus our Lord" (2 Timothy 1:2 ERV). Later Paul adds:

> I always remember you in my prayers day and night. And in these prayers I thank God for you. He is the God my ancestors served, and I have always served him with a clear conscience. I remember that you cried for me. I want very much to see you so that I can be filled with joy. I remember your true faith. That kind of faith first belonged to your grandmother Lois and to your mother Eunice. I know you now have the same faith. (2 Timothy 1:3–5 ERV)

Thus, Timothy became a spiritual son of Paul as Mark was a spiritual son of Peter.

Paul first met Timothy after his separation from Mark and Barnabas. Paul had traveled to certain cities of Turkey or Asia Minor where he and Timothy met. By this time Paul had chosen Silas or Silvanus to travel with him. In Acts 15, the writer Luke states that believers in Antioch put Paul into the Lord's care and sent him out. Paul and Silas go through the countries of Syria and Cilicia, helping the churches grow stronger. In Acts 16:1 (ERV), Luke writes, "Paul went to the city of Derbe and then to Lystra, where a follower of Jesus named Timothy lived."

At this point several important things are learned about Timothy. Like John Mark, Timothy had a very strong religious background. He appeared to be ready to do mission work. Paul treated him as a young companion. There seemed to be no problems from family ties as Timothy traveled to Macedonia in the northern part of Greece. At the city of Troas, Luke the physician and historian joined the group. Luke and Timothy apparently escaped the persecution in Philippi that included the beating and incarceration of Paul and Silas. They also avoided similar problems in Thessalonica. In the city of Berea, the church at this location sent Paul away to the coast for his own protection from persecutors in Berea and Thessalonica. Then Luke mentioned, "So the believers immediately sent Paul away to the coast, but Silas and Timothy stayed in Berea" (Acts 17:14 ERV).

When Paul came to the city of Athens, he sent a message for Silas and Timothy to come and join him as soon as they could (Acts 17:15). Thus, it can be seen that Timothy was not afraid of the missionary journey, but he was certainly not preaching or being physically presented. Silas seemed to be an older companion and, in a real way, his protector. Paul was bearing the brunt of the physical punishment. Later Luke revealed that Silas and Timothy met Paul in Corinth. Paul eventually stayed there for a year and a half teaching the gospel.

An assumption can be made that Timothy traveled with Paul to such places as Cenchrea, Caesarea, Antioch, Galatia, Phrygia, and Ephesus. In Acts 19 Luke writes about Paul: "He planned to go through the regions of Macedonia and Achaia, and then go to Jerusalem. He thought, 'After I visit Jerusalem, I must also visit Rome.' Timothy and Erastus were two of his helpers. Paul sent them ahead to Macedonia. But he stayed in Asia for a while" (Acts 19:21–22 ERV).

After Acts 10, Luke does not mention Timothy and his travels any more. The picture given is of a young Christian gaining maturity and promise. Timothy may have returned home at some time, but the scriptures are silent. The rest of his stay must be found in the letters of Paul.

At this point, it would be good to review the effect of Silas on Timothy. While being left in Macedonia, Silas and Timothy most likely ministered to the Christians in that area. It may be assumed that Silas was the older of the two and guided Timothy in the mission work in that area.

The church in Philippi was diverse in nature. The house of Lydia would have been quite influential with the wealth that was part of Lydia's businesses. She had likely become rich selling her purple dye to merchants in the Mediterranean area. Her home would have been large enough to hold the meetings of the church. Her business sprang from her early days in Thyatira in modern Turkey. The purple dye came from shellfish and the cloth stained by the dye was worn by the wealthy.

Lydia had been a worshiper of God and became the first convert to Christianity in Europe. When the church at Philippi met at the house of Lydia, it may be remembered that Silas and Timothy were there. This group would include the young woman who had the evil spirit cast out and the jailer who had imprisoned Paul and Silas. Thus, Paul and Silas were worshiping with former enemies. Paul had cast out this spirit of fortune-telling from the young woman. The woman was a slave, and her owners made a great deal of money from the predictions she made while possessed with the evil fortune-telling spirit. This caused a revolt among the owners, and they had Paul and Silas cast into prison.

The magistrates, who were Romans, listened to the complaints and ordered the beating of Paul and Silas. There is a strong element of antisemitic conduct here as the accusers identify Paul and Silas as Jews while they are Romans. The jailer, who was now a Christian, must have participated in the severe beating that was administered to Paul and Silas. The jailer may have remembered the confusion when an earthquake shook the jail and freed the prisoners. He may also have remembered that he heard the singing and praying of Paul and Silas. He also may have mentioned that he was about to fall on his sword but was stopped by Paul. It can be imagined that Silas and Timothy heard this story many times while they were staying in Philippi. Timothy's faith must have been strengthened. He had been in the company of Paul and Silas, but not a prisoner.

Silas must have confirmed the events and again related the baptism of the jailer and his family. Silas may have told the story of their journey to Lydia's house after this ordeal. Acts 16:40 (NIV) states that "after Paul and Silas came out of the prison, they went to Lydia's house, where they met with the brothers and sisters and encouraged them. Then they left." Timothy no doubt listened to these remembrances many times and was greatly influenced by the courage of his companions and the conversion of this diverse group.

The young woman freed from the evil spirit must have been there to relate her story. Timothy's stay in Philippi would have strengthened his faith. After staying in Philippi, they remained in Macedonia and may have revisited Thessalonica. Acts 17 recalls the events that had taken place in Thessalonica:

> But the Jews were jealous and taking some wicked men of the rabble, they formed a mob, set the city in an uproar, and attacked the house of Jason, seeking to bring them out to the crowd. And when they could not find them, they dragged Jason and some of the brothers before the city authorities shouting, "These men who have turned the world upside down have come here also, and Jason has received them, and they are all acting against the decrees of Caesar, saying that there is another king, Jesus." And the people and the city authorities were disturbed when they heard these things. And when they had taken money as security for Jason and the rest, they let them go. (Acts 17:5–9 ESV)

F. F. Bruce writes that Paul and Silas had suffered persecution in Philippi because they were the natural targets for antisemitic anger from a Gentile city. He notes, "Luke was a Gentile and Timothy a half-Gentile." Bruce further shows the irony of the situation in that after the release of Paul and Silas, Paul being a Roman citizen, demanded an apology. The praetors had to come in person and apologize to them, but even so they requested them to move on. The responsibility of protecting two unpopular Roman citizens was more than they felt able to bear.[27]

Thessalonica seemed friendlier to the missionaries until problems arose with certain Jewish leaders. Bruce adds, "Paul's Thessalonian friends got him safely away by night to Berea, a city about 60 miles west by southwest of Thessalonica; from there he was escorted to Athens. In Athens he was rejoined by Silas and Timothy, whom he immediately sent back to Macedonia."[28]

The stay in Berea must have been a time of relief for Timothy. He was with truth seekers who studied the scriptures. After time spent there and his eventual return to Thessalonica and Philippi, Timothy was a veteran of the missionary journey. While not enduring any physical harm himself, he had no doubt witnessed the sufferings of Paul and of his companion Silas. Timothy had seen the persecutions of Jason in Thessalonica. He must have known by this time that Christianity could cause extreme danger to the believers. Timothy did not turn back to his home but stayed with Silas to await further instructions. These instructions were to come by Paul to Corinth. Paul did not mention his great disappointment in the reception at Athens when he summoned Timothy and Silas. Likely, his experience became known to Timothy who would recognize that not every community would have believers like Lydia.

Corinth must have been an eye opener for young Timothy because of its immorality. He eventually met a wonderful couple called Aquila and Priscilla who "had recently moved to Corinth from Italy. They left Italy because Claudius had given an order for all the Jews to leave Rome. Paul went to visit Aquila and Priscilla. They were tentmakers, the same as Paul, so he stayed with them and worked with them" (Acts 18:2–3 ERV).

Luke then talks about Silas and Timothy joining the group of Christians in Corinth, coming from Macedonia. This addition of Timothy and Silas must have helped relieve Paul of certain duties for Luke writes, "Paul spent all his time telling God's message" (Acts 18:5 ERV). Paul was disappointed at first in his work in Corinth, but a vision from God encouraged him to continue his message there as the Lord tells Paul, "Don't be afraid, and don't stop talking to people. I am with you, and no one will be able to hurt you. Many of my people are in this city" (Acts 18:9–11 ERV). This vision encouraged Paul to stay for a year and a half, continuing to teach God's message.

After the vision, certain Jews tried (unsuccessfully) to disrupt Paul's work by taking him to court. The judge, named Gallio, was governor of the province of Achaia where Corinth was located. Gallio was a Roman and little interested in the accusation of the Jews:

> Paul was ready to say something, but Gallio spoke to the Jews. He said, "I would listen to you if your complaint was about a crime or other wrong. But it is only about words and names, arguments about your own law. So you must solve this problem yourselves. I don't want to be a judge of this matter." So Gallio made them leave the court. (Acts 18:14–16 ERV)

Paul was rescued by Gallio. Bruce reminds us that Gallio came from well-known Roman family who was of Spanish origin. Gallio's father was Marcus Annaeus Seneca (who was a distinguished professor of rhetoric), and his older brother was Lucius Annaeus Seneca (Stoic philosopher and tutor to the future Emperor Nero). His family name changed because of his adoptions as heir by his father's friend, Lucius Junius Gallio.[29]

Along with Paul, Silas, Aquila, and Priscilla, Timothy probably became optimistic, believing the vision of encouragement to Paul meant that the gospel could be preached without fear of persecution. Priscilla and Aquila were enthusiastic missionaries. They eventually went with Paul to Ephesus and influenced Apollos while he was at Ephesus. Apollos was a learned and eloquent man:

> He had been taught about the Lord and was always excited to talk to people about Jesus. What he taught was right, but the only baptism he knew about was the baptism that John taught. Apollos began to speak very boldly in the synagogue. When Priscilla and Aquila heard him speak, they took him home and helped him understand the way of God better. (Acts 18:25–26 ERV)

As they were going on, Timothy and Erastus accompanied Paul, Aquila, and Priscilla to Ephesus. Erastus was an interesting convert from Corinth. Bruce writes:

> On April 15, 1929, archaeologists based on the American School at Athens uncovered in Old Corinth a slab bearing a Latin inscription which should probably be rendered: "Erastus, in consideration of his *aedileship*, laid this pavement at his own expense." The possibility—some say probability—must be recognized that the Erastus of

the inscription is identical with Paul's Corinthian friend; if so, his service as city treasurer (the post which he was occupying at the beginning of A. D. 57) proved so satisfactory that some twenty years later he was promoted to the dignity of *aedile* (curator of public works).[30]

Timothy may have had contact with Erastus, Apollos, and Aquila and Priscilla during his stay in Corinth. Timothy was to be introduced to various factions in the Corinthian church. Such conditions would have been something new. He had seen persecution toward Paul at Philippi and Thessalonika, but dissension in the church body itself would have been different. Also, Paul had been informed of a group in Corinth who invoked the name of Peter.

Bruce, thinking Peter may have visited Corinth, writes:

> Had Peter paid a visit to Corinth in Paul's absence? This is possible: Peter seems, from about A.D. 50 onwards, to have embarked on a more widespread ministry than hitherto, concentrating probably in accordance with the Jerusalem leaders' agreement with Paul and Barnabas on Jewish communities in various centres. If he visited the synagogue in Corinth, he would no doubt also have greeted the church there, which included converts from Judaism as well as from paganism. We have already remarked on the impossibility of maintaining a clear line of demarcation between the Jewish and the Gentile mission fields, and on the opportunities of misunderstanding which were liable to arise between the two parties to the agreement. Apollos was a free agent with no apostolic status, and his activity in Corinth or any part of Paul's mission-field presented no threat to Paul's authority, but it was

different with Peter. Doubt could easily have been the case on Paul's commission by anyone who was so minded—he had received it by his own account, in a vision shared by no one else, whereas Peter's apostolic credentials were unquestionable. If he said something which differed from Paul's teaching, which was more likely to be right?[31]

Timothy was to add another influence upon Paul's spiritual experience. Thus, it may easily be said that Corinth was a maturation experience for him. He chose to remain aligned with Paul although this would not exclude his admiration for Silas, Aquila, Priscilla, Apollos, Erastus, and Peter. He certainly would have remembered Jason, Crispus, and perhaps the decision of Gallio.

Soon Paul would leave Corinth for Antioch and points east including Caesarea, Jerusalem, and Cenchrea. Timothy, as seen in the writings of Luke, eventually went back to Macedonia and probably Corinth with Silas. Apollos came to Corinth and very likely influenced Timothy with his eloquence and devotion. Luke records that when Apollos "arrived there, he was a great help to those who had believed in Jesus because of God's grace. He used the Scripture and showed that Jesus is the Messiah" (Acts 18:27–28 ERV).

To follow Timothy from his time in Corinth to the later years, we can read the letters of Paul that mention him and the Pastoral Epistles to complete our knowledge of this outstanding younger Christian man. Luke mentions that Timothy and a host of disciples joined Paul for another journey. The *ISBE* explains:

Among the traveling companions who joined Paul in Corinth, or this Aegean port of Cenchrea, ready to sail with him to Judea, Luke mentions Sopater

of Berea, the son of Pyrrhus; Aristarchus and Se-
cundus from Thessalonica; Gaius of Derbe and
Timothy (originally from Lystra), and Tychicus and
Trophimus from the province of Asia (the latter of
whom was a Gentile Christian from Ephesus).[32]

Timothy is mentioned as being in Troas and probably all the way
to Miletus and in so doing bypassed Ephesus. Paul was in a hurry
to get to Jerusalem for Pentecost. Luke records Paul's meeting
with the elders of Ephesus at Miletus, and it can be assumed that
Timothy was a witness to the farewell speech of Paul to the elders
of Ephesus.

Did Timothy continue his journey with Paul? Luke in recording
the journey includes stops at Tyre and Caesarea as well as the is-
lands of Cos and Rhodes. At Caesarea they visited Phillip. Again,
it is unclear whether Timothy went to Jerusalem. Timothy may
have been there. The *ISBE* states that the friends of Paul "eventually reached Jerusalem where Paul was apprehended. This of
course terminated, for the time, his apostolic journeys, but not
the cooperation of his friends, or of Timothy among them."[33]

Paul, after a successful appeal to Caesar, eventually went to
Rome. Timothy, however, is mentioned in Paul's greetings to the
Thessalonians which would have been written much earlier. The
so-called prior letters of Paul find Timothy as a companion. In
his letter to the Colossians, Paul included both John Mark and
Timothy with him in Rome where most scholars locate the origin
of the letter. Bruce writes:

> But if this letter was indeed sent from Rome it is
> necessary to take account of the implication of the
> final greetings in which Paul names Aristarchus,
> Mark (the cousin of Barnabas) and Jesus surnamed

Justus as the only men of Jewish birth who are with him at the time as 'fellow-workers for the kingdom of God'—men, he adds, who 'have been a comfort to me' [Colossians 4:10]. He has other companions who are of Gentile origin, but no other 'men of the circumcision' apart from Timothy, whose name is coupled with his own in the initial salutation of the letter.[34]

Paul's influence was great. The range of his friendship and the warmth of his affection are qualities which no attentive reader of his letters can miss. There are scores of people mentioned in the New Testament who are known to us, by name at least, simply because they were friends of Paul. And in his friends, he was able to call forth a devotion which knew no limits. Paul acknowledged Timothy as the closest of friends.

Priscilla and Aquilla risked their lives for Paul in a dangerous situation. Epaphroditis of Philippi overtaxed his strength and suffered an almost fatal illness in his anxiety to be of service to the imprisoned apostle. Timothy readily surrendered whatever personal ambitions he might have cherished to play the part of a son to Paul and help him in his missionary activity, showing a selfless concern for others that matched the apostle's own eagerness to spend and be spent for them.

Timothy is found in the letters of Paul. He is mentioned in 1 Thessalonians: "Greetings from Paul, Silas and Timothy. To the church of those in Thessalonica, who are in God the Father and the Lord Jesus Christ" (1 Thessalonians 1:1 ERV). Most scholars believe this was Paul's first letter and was written from Corinth. Whether Timothy helped in the actual writing of this letter is speculative.

Timothy is also mentioned in 2 Thessalonians 1:1 (ERV): "Greetings from Paul, Silas, and Timothy. To the church of those in Thessalonica, who are in God our Father and the Lord Jesus Christ." This letter is believed to have been written shortly after 1 Thessalonians to clear up doctrinal issues such as the Parousia.

In 1 Corinthians, Timothy is found in Ephesus with Paul. Paul writes:

> Timothy might come to you. Try to make him feel comfortable with you. He is working for the Lord the same as I am. So none of you should refuse to accept Timothy. Help him continue on his trip in peace so that he can come back to me. I am expecting him to come back with the other brothers. Now about our brother Apollos: I strongly encouraged him to visit you with the other brothers. He prefers not to come now, but he will come when he has the opportunity. (1 Corinthians 16:10–12 ERV)

Thus, Timothy was encouraged to go back to Corinth, with Apollos coming later. Timothy was seen as one of the next generation to carry on the gospel message in Corinth, along with Apollos. At this time Priscilla and Aquila had already started a church home in Ephesus and only sent greetings to the Corinthians.

In 2 Corinthians Paul appears to write the Corinthians about leaving Ephesus:

> When we came into Macedonia, we had no rest. We found trouble all around us. We had fighting on the outside and fear on the inside. But God encourages those who are troubled, and he certainly

encouraged us by bringing Titus to us. It was so good to see him, but we were encouraged even more to hear about the encouragement you gave him. He told us that you really want to see me and that you are very sorry for what you did. And he told us how ready and willing you are to help me. When I heard this, I was so much happier. (2 Corinthians 7:5–7 ERV)

Since Timothy is mentioned in the greetings as being with Paul, it can be assumed that Titus was reunited with Paul and Timothy in Macedonia. Later on Paul promises to visit the Corinthians for the third time, and it can be assumed that Timothy was his companion.

In the so-called prison epistles, Timothy is mentioned by Paul. In Philippi, Paul greets his readers, "Greetings from Paul and Timothy, servants of Jesus Christ. To all of you in Philippi who are God's holy people in Christ Jesus, including your elders and special servants" (Philippians 1:1 ERV).

In Colossians, Paul greets that church in this way, "Greetings from Paul, an apostle of Christ Jesus. I am an apostle because that is what God wanted. Greetings from Timothy, our brother in Christ. To the holy and faithful brothers and sisters in Christ who live in Colossae" (Colossians 1:1–2 ERV).

Paul is more specific when he writes Philemon. He is in prison with Timothy and others. Paul's greeting states, "Greetings from Paul, a prisoner for Jesus Christ, and from Timothy, our brother. To Philemon, our dear friend and worker with us. Also, to our sister Apphia, to Archippus, who serves with us in the Lord's army, and to the church that meets in your home" (Philemon 1:1–2 ERV). Paul also mentions a fellow prisoner Epaphras and then Mark, Aristarchus, Demas, and Luke (Philemon 1:23–24).

Timothy and Mark, who are referred to as sons by Paul and Peter, are working together. In addition, in Philemon, Paul counts Onesimus as a spiritual son. He asks Philemon's assistance in accepting Philemon's slave as a brother in Christ. "I am asking you for my son Onesimus. He became my son while I was in prison" (Philemon 1:10 ERV).

Where was Paul in prison when he wrote these letters? The commentator A. S. Peake writes in *The Expositor's Greek Testament, Colossians* that "since Paul was a prisoner when he wrote it, our only alternatives are Caesarea and Rome." Peake says it's probably best to stick with the common view that Colossians should be dated during the early part of Paul's Roman imprisonment.[35] It also seems that Caesarea was a very involved time for Paul who was preparing for his defense before Felix, Festus, and Agrippa. Timothy seems not to have been with Paul at Caesarea.

An interesting reference to Timothy appears in Hebrews 13:23 when the writer of Hebrews indicates that Timothy has been released. In his commentary *The Expositor's Greek Testament*, Marcus Dods comments: "Evidently Timothy had been under arrest; where, when, or why is not known."[36] Obviously the writer of Hebrews knew Timothy as well as Paul, Apollos, and Luke among others. The place where Timothy was imprisoned most likely was Ephesus or Rome but remains unclear. The only conclusion that can safely be drawn is that Timothy also suffered imprisonment as did Paul, Silas, and other Christians.

The maturation of Timothy is found in Paul's letters to him. Here we see the transfer of responsibility from men like Paul or Peter to younger men, including Timothy and Mark. Both 1 Timothy and 2 Timothy were certainly Paul's last letters. They are filled with advice, comfort, specific duties for Timothy, and a general feeling of father to son love.

Paul, having been rescued from the power of the Sanhedrin by the Roman officer Lysias, now faced a series of trials before Roman authorities. Paul stood in the court of a governor named Felix. The Sanhedrin had brought their lawyer Tertullus. After making complimentary statements before Felix, Tertullus charged Paul with being a nuisance, a ringleader of a sect, and a profaner of the temple. All these charges were met with doubt by Felix. In his commentary, Rackham states:

> There was no evidence whatever against him. His real crime was simply that he was a consistent Christian. Felix, owing to his residence in Palestine, had for a Roman a very accurate knowledge of this new way, and he perceived this. He knew also that this was no real crime. The other Christians were left unmolested even by the Jews, and Paul ought to have been set free.[37]

When Felix heard Paul's defense for a second time, (he had adjourned the first defense), he brought his wife Drusilla, who was Jewish. She was the daughter of Herod Agrippa who had executed James and intended to execute Peter. She had abandoned her first husband for Felix. When giving his defense, Paul, as had John the Baptist, reasoned about very serious matters, righteousness, temperance, and the judgment to come (Acts 24:24–25).

Felix soon was replaced by Festus, a governor with little knowledge of Jewish customs. However, he saw that Paul posed no real threat against Caesar. At this time, Paul's future was sealed by his appeal to Caesar (*Caesarem appelo*). Festus conferred with his Roman court who were his legal advisors. The answer was, "to Caesar you shall go" (Acts 25:12 ESV).

Paul appeared before Herod Agrippa in his final trial. This was at the request of Festus. Luke records the visit:

> Now when certain days were passed, Agrippa the king and Bernice arrived at Caesarea, and saluted Festus. And as they tarried there many days, Festus laid Paul's case before the king, saying, there is a certain man left a prisoner by Felix, about whom, when I was at Jerusalem, the chief priests and the elders of the Jews informed me, asking for sentence against him. To whom I answered, that it is not the custom of the Romans to give up any man, before that the accused have the accusers face to face, and have had opportunity to make his defense concerning the matter laid against him. When therefore they were come together here, I made no delay, but on the next day sat down on the judgment-seat and commanded the man to be brought. Concerning whom, when the accusers stood up, they brought no charge of such evil things as I supposed; but had certain questions against him of their own religion, and of one Jesus, who was dead, whom Paul affirmed to be alive. And I, being perplexed how to inquire concerning these things, asked whether he would go to Jerusalem and there to be judged of these matters. But when Paul had appealed to be kept for the decision of the emperor, I commanded him to be kept till I should send him to Caesar. And Agrippa said unto Festus, I also could wish to hear the man myself. (Acts 25:13–22 ASV)

Paul's appearance before Agrippa II and his sister Bernice was accompanied with much pomp. The Roman military was there and the leading citizens of Caesarea. Bruce in his commentary states that Paul engaged in an *"apologia pro vita sua"* before

Agrippa.[38] It is perhaps his greatest oration. He began with praise for Agrippa and his knowledge of Jewish customs. Of course, this relieved Festus who had no Jewish background while Agrippa could trace his lineage back to Herod the Great.

Paul recounts his own personal history as a Pharisee and as a persecutor of Christians. He astounds his audience with a recounting of a vision on the way to Damascus. All this perplexed Festus, especially the part about resurrection. He interrupted Paul's defense with a shout that Paul is insane. Paul's appeal to Agrippa was persuasive, even appealing to his knowledge of Judaism. As Bruce notes, Agrippa has quite a dilemma. "If he says 'yes', he suddenly realizes that he is being maneuvered into a position of public agreement with Paul; academic interest is one thing, but confession of Christianity quite another. 'In short you are trying to persuade me to act the Christian.'"[39]

All of Paul's statements in his defense before Felix, Festus, and Agrippa came to one conclusion for these judges. Paul was innocent, but he had appealed to Caesar. His wish was granted, and the outcome was to be monumental. The rest of Luke's account in Acts focuses on Paul's dangerous journey to Rome. He faced shipwreck and landed on Malta. He was to have success there before reaching Italy. He was greeted on his way to Rome by Christians from the city. After leaving the place called Three Taverns, he enters the city of Rome. As Rackham describes, "The apostle for the first time trod the streets and viewed the buildings of the Eternal City, the Mistress of the World, the Babylon on the Seven Hills."[40]

As Luke concludes, "And he abode two whole years in his own hired dwelling and received all that went in unto him, preaching the kingdom of God, and teaching the things concerning the Lord Jesus Christ with all boldness, none forbidding" (Acts 28:30–31 ASV).

In Rackham's commentary on Acts, he makes this statement about Paul in Rome: "Unfortunately the more light we get, the more difficult does it become to restore the exact history of events."[41] Paul during the two years of his stay in Rome was under house arrest—in his own dwelling and free to write letters to the Ephesians, Colossians, Philippians, and Philemon. The imprisonment was a great reward to future generations as it gave him time to compose these great letters.

During this prison stay, Paul is reunited with Timothy and Mark. Also with Paul were Luke and Demas and visitors such as Tychicus, Epaphras, and Epaphroditus. A runaway slave, Onesimus, found Paul and thus returned a different person to his owner Philemon. Paul was eventually released and perhaps makes a trip to Spain.

After visits to Greece, Crete, Ephesus, and Macedonia, Paul reached Rome again where he was imprisoned. Rackham notes that at some point he wrote to Timothy. "The apostle knows that the end is at hand, and he is conscious that he is writing his last words (2 Timothy). His apprehensions were fulfilled. Whether Timothy arrives in time we do not know."[42]

At this point the best sources of connecting the father and son relationship is Paul's second letter to Timothy. Paul begins the letter by remembering the life of Timothy from his earliest days:

> I remember your true faith. That kind of faith first belonged to your grandmother Lois and to your mother Eunice. I know you now have the same faith. That is why I want you to remember the gift God gave you. God gave you that gift when I laid my hands on you. Now I want you to use that gift and let it grow more and more, like a small flame grows into a fire. The Spirit God gave us does not

make us afraid. His Spirit is our source of power and love and self-control. So don't be ashamed to tell people about our Lord Jesus. And don't be ashamed of me—I am in prison for the Lord. But suffer with me for the Good News. God gives us the strength to do that. (2 Timothy 1:5–8 ERV)

Paul then adds:

God saved us and chose us to be his holy people, but not because of any thing we ourselves did. God saved us and made us his people because that was what he wanted and because of his grace. That grace was given to us through Christ Jesus before time began. And now it has been shown to us in the coming of our Savior Christ Jesus. He destroyed death and showed us the way to have life. Yes, through the Good News Jesus showed us the way to have life that cannot be destroyed. (2 Timothy 1:9–10 ERV)

This letter by Paul to Timothy signifies a passing of the torch. The letter was replete with practical advice for Timothy. Paul admonished, "As a servant of the Lord, you must not argue. You must be kind to everyone. You must be a good teacher, and you must be patient. You must gently teach those who don't agree with you" (2 Timothy 2:24–25 ERV). Paul continued to admonish Timothy when he wrote:

But you should continue following the teaching you learned. You know it is true, because you know you can trust those who taught you. You have known the Holy Scriptures since you were a child. These scriptures are able to make you wise. And that wisdom leads to salvation through faith in Christ Jesus. All scripture is given by God. And all Scripture is useful for teaching and for showing people what is wrong in their lives. It is useful for correcting faults and teaching the right way to live. Using the Scriptures, those who serve God will be prepared and will have everything they need to do every good work. (2 Timothy 3:14–17 ERV)

The letter told Timothy that Paul saw the nearing end of his life on earth:

I have fought the good fight. I have finished the race. I have served the Lord faithfully. Now, a prize is waiting for me—the crown that will show I am right with God. The Lord, the judge who judges rightly, will give it to me on the Day. Yes, he will give it to me and to everyone else who is eagerly looking forward to his coming. (2 Timothy 4:7–8 ERV)

This letter showed a relationship that Paul had nourished in his love for Timothy. Paul never admitted that he needed a successor, and he did not specifically name Timothy. However, he urgently requested Timothy to come to him and asks him to bring Mark with him to help in the work (2 Timothy 4:11). Rackham states that it is impossible to know if Timothy arrived. Tradition revealed Paul was executed on the Ostian Way in 64–65 A.D. "Tradition marks the spot at the Abbey of Tre Fontane, three miles from the city gate; and his body was laid where now stands the Church of S. Paulo Fuori le Mura (without the walls)."[43]

A great deal of speculation surrounds Peter's last days. Rackham theorizes that Peter was executed in Rome as he was "discovered by the authorities; and not being a Roman citizen, he was put to death by crucifixion in the Vatican gardens beyond the Tiber. If this happened in 67 or early 68, it would account for the date assigned to the martyrdom of both apostles by Eusebius."[44] The quote from Clement, the bishop of Rome, states:

> Let us set before our eyes the good apostles. There was Peter who by reason of unrighteous jealousy endured not one nor two but many labours, and thus having bourne his testimony went to his appointed place of glory. By reason of jealousy and strife Paul by his example pointed out the prize of patient endurance. After that he had been seven times in bonds, had been driven into exile, had been stoned, had preached in the East and in the West, he won the noble renown which was the reward of his faith, having taught righteousness unto the whole world and having reached the farthest boundary of the West; and when he had borne his testimony before the rulers, so departed from the world and went unto the holy place, having been found a notable pattern of patient endurance.[45]

The future of Timothy and his companion Mark were not told in the scriptures. Peter did not appoint a successor, and Paul did not either. From scriptural references, Mark seemed to be older than Timothy. The apostle John did not mention either one in his letter. John would have been in Ephesus around 70 A.D. At the same time both Timothy and Mark may have elected to stay in Rome. The Roman church became the leading church and Peter was given more prominence than Paul.

TITUS AND OTHERS

Paul had spiritually adopted another son besides Timothy. In Titus 1:4 (ERV), Paul addressed Titus as "a true son to me in the faith we share together." Titus was assigned work in Crete just as Timothy had worked mainly in Asia Minor. Titus's instructions were similar. When troubles arose, Titus was given authority by Paul to correct them. "You have full authority to do this, so don't let anyone think that they can ignore you" (Titus 2:15 ERV).

Much of what Paul wrote to Titus reminds the reader of his admonition to Timothy. Paul reflected on the power of grace:

> This is the way we should live, because God's grace has come. That grace can save everyone. It teaches us not to live against God and not to do the bad things the world wants to do. It teaches us to live on earth now in a wise and right way—a way that shows true devotion to God. We should live like

that while we are waiting for the coming of our great God and Saviour Jesus Christ. He is our great hope, and he will come with glory. He gave himself for us. He died to free us from all evil. He died to make us pure—people who belong only to him and who always want to be good. These are the things you should tell people. Encourage them, and when they are wrong, correct them. You have full authority to do this, so don't let anyone think they can ignore you. (Titus 2:11–15 ERV)

Paul also reminded Titus of the power of the Holy Spirit:

He saved us through the washing that made us new people. He saved us by making us new through the Holy Spirit. God poured out to us that Holy Spirit fully through Jesus Christ our Savior. We were made right with God by his grace. God saved us so that we could be his children and look forward to receiving life that never ends. This is a true statement. (Titus 3:5–6 ERV)

Titus was a companion of Artemus and Tychicus as well as Zenas and Apollos. He, like Timothy, was instructed to help these Christians. Paul's charge to Titus was clear: "Be sure that they have everything they need. Our people must learn to use their lives for doing good and helping anyone who has a need. Then they will not have empty lives" (Titus 3:13–14 ERV).

John Rutherford refers to Titus in an article in the *International Standard Bible Encyclopedia* as "one of Paul's very dear and trusted friends, and the fact that he was chosen by the apostle to act as his delegate to Corinth to transact difficult and delicate work in the church there and that he did this oftener than once, and did it thoroughly and successfully showed what a capable and resourceful servant he was."[46]

Titus, from all indications, stayed in Crete. No doubt he had success there as he did in Corinth. Paul lavishes praise on this true son in his statement in 2 Corinthians:

> Now about Titus—he is my partner. He is working together with me to help you. And about the other brothers—they are sent from the churches, and they bring glory to Christ. So show these men that you really have love. Show them why we are proud of you. Then all the churches can see it. (2 Corinthians 8:23–24 ERV)

Paul and Peter would use the word *children* often in their writings. The Apostle John also used *children* many times in his letters. Paul uses the word *son* in his personal letter to Philemon when he writes about a runaway slave. Paul is not writing about a privileged Christian such as Timothy or Mark, but about Onesimus. The word here for child, *teknos*, is masculine in this case because it refers to a particular male.[47]

As Paul was writing from his first imprisonment, he could be writing from Caesarea or Rome. He included Timothy in his greetings. Onesimus had escaped his servitude from the home of Philemon and found his way to Paul with whom he found an enduring bond. As he noted in a play on the name of Onesimus, the runaway has become useful not useless. He wrote, "In the past he was useless to you. But now he has become useful for both you and me" (Philemon 1:11 ERV).

Evidently Paul knew Philemon, Apphia, and Archippus and the home church where they met. He praised the household and the church, which was situated in the Colossae region. In the very essence of tact, Paul asked Philemon to graciously receive Onesimus who had served as a son to the older apostle who needed help. It can be safely assumed that Onesimus became a child of God while visiting Paul and that he served him well. The question of his running away remains a mystery as does why he found Paul.

Paul did not defend or condemn Onesimus. As he wrote:

> I am sending him back to you, but it's as hard as losing part of myself. I would like to keep him here to help me while I am still in prison for telling the Good News. By helping me here, he would be representing you. But I did not want to do anything without asking you first. Then whatever you do for me will be what you want to do, not what I forced you to do. Onesimus was separated from you for a short time. Maybe that happened so that you could have him back forever, not to be just a slave, but better than a slave, to be a dear brother. That's what he is to me. And I know he will be even more so to you, both as your slave and as one who shares your faith in the Lord. (Philemon 12–16 ERV)

The book of Philemon ends on an optimistic tone as Paul was very sure that his request would be fulfilled and that Onesimus would be accepted back as a Christian brother. He was filled with encouragement as he expected to visit Philemon upon his release from prison. Onesimus thus became another son of Paul and in his own way helped Paul for a brief period.

Personal connections are varied with Peter and Paul. That Peter was married is known because Jesus heals his mother-in-law (Matthew 8:14). Paul refers to Peter's being married in I Corinthians 9:5 (ERV): "We have the right to bring a believing wife with us when we travel, don't we? The other apostles and the Lord's brothers and Peter all do this."

Paul used the expression *sister* in Romans 16:1 when he speaks of Phoebe as a "sister in Christ." Andronicus and Junia were called his relatives who were in prison with him (Romans 16:7). Other relatives mentioned by Paul in Romans 16 include Herodion, Asyncritus, Phlegon, Hermas, Patrobas, Hermes, Lucius, Jason, Sosipater, and Quartus. The best translation of *relative* is countryman, or kinsman in the spiritual sense. All who are mentioned do not have the relationship of Timothy who was called a *son*. And Peter's mother-in-law does not appear prominent in Paul's ministry as Mark's mother did.

The apostle John, who survived longer than Paul or Peter, mentioned his children but chose no one as his spiritual son. John's closest brother is a dear friend Gaius. "To my dear friend Gaius, a person I truly love" (3 John 1). John's second letter is addressed to a lady chosen of God and to her children. Most scholars take the word *lady to* refer to a church and her children as members of that church.

The conclusion must be reached that only Mark and Timothy qualify as the closest sons of Peter and Paul. Others might be children or brothers, but the relationship of these two is sustained by the church historian Eusebius Pamphilus who was Bishop of Caesarea. Eusebius writes that the church at Rome "persevered in every variety of entreaties to solicit Mark as the companion of Peter, and whose gospel we have, to leave them a monument of the doctrine thus orally communicated, in writing. Nor did they cease their solicitations until they had prevailed with the men and thus become the means of that history which is called the Gospel according to Mark."[48]

According to Eusebius, Mark went to Egypt and proclaimed the gospel there which he had written. While there he "established churches at the city of Alexandria."[49] Eusebius also states that, under the rule of Nero, both Paul and Peter were executed. "Paul is therefore said to have been beheaded at Rome, and Peter to have been crucified under him. And this account is confirmed by the fact that the names of Peter and Paul still remain in the cemeteries of that city even to this day."[50]

Eusebius relates that "Timothy, indeed, is recorded as having first received the episcopate at Ephesus, *en Epheso paroikos*, as Titus also was appointed over the churches in Crete."[51] In closing remarks about Mark, Eusebius refers to Clement, an early scholar of the first century. Clement of Rome says the Christians of Rome requested that Mark write a gospel:

> When Peter had proclaimed the word publicly at Rome and declared the gospel under the influence of the spirit; as there was a great number present, they requested Mark who had followed him from afar, and remembered well what he had said, to reduce these things in writing, and that after composing the gospel he give it to those who requested it of him.[52]

Clement also stated that the last gospel was written by John the Apostle and was a "spiritual gospel."[53]

The study of Mark and Timothy reminds us that Peter and Paul had spiritual relatives through Christ. In Romans 16, Paul listed several relatives, even a woman who had become as a mother to him. Peter advised his readers to love all the "brothers and sisters in God's family" (1 Peter 2:19 ERV). He encouraged those who were persecuted that "you know that your brothers and sisters all over the world are having the same suffering that you have" (1 Peter 5:9 ERV).

In his second letter, Peter continued to address "my brothers and sisters" as he told them "God called you and chose you to be his" (2 Peter 1:10 ERV). Peter and John the Apostle were very close as brothers in Christ. They began this ministry as recorded in Acts 3. The scriptures tell that the Jewish leaders saw that Peter and John had been with Jesus (Acts 4:13).

Paul had a special brother and sister in Aquila and Priscilla. They are mentioned several times by Paul when they were at various cities. In 1 Corinthians they are mentioned by Paul: "The churches in Asia send you their greetings. Aquila and Priscilla greet you in the Lord. Also the church that meets in their house sends greetings. All the brothers and sisters send their greetings" (1 Corinthians 16:19–20 ERV). Priscilla and Aquila are also found in Rome where Paul mentions them in Romans:

> Give my greetings to Priscilla and Aquila, who have worked together with me for Christ Jesus. They risked their own lives to save mine. I am thankful to them, and all the non-Jewish churches are thankful to them. Also, give greetings to the church that meets in their house. (Romans 16:3–5 ERV)

Paul also met this Christian couple in Corinth. In the book of Acts it is written:

> Later, Paul left Athens and went to the city of Corinth. There he met a Jewish man named Aquila, who was born in the country of Pontus. But he and his wife, Priscilla, had recently moved to

Corinth from Italy. They left Italy because Claudius had given an order for all Jews to leave Rome. Paul went to visit Aquila and Priscilla. They were tentmakers, the same as Paul, so he stayed with them and worked with them. (Acts 18:1–3 ERV)

While the aforementioned persons were brothers and sisters of Peter and Paul respectively, only Mark and Timothy play the important role of permanent sons for these giants of the faith. Their progress in the history of the early church is evident. History, which is beyond the scriptures, confirms that both Mark and Timothy became leaders in the spread of Christianity. Less is known of Titus, but the scriptures leave him in Crete to fortify the Christians there.

Legacy is very important in the success of the gospel message. The church prospers when succession of leadership is apparent. The sons of the apostles confirm this truth.

ADDENDUM

A word study of *son* is appropriate. In his acknowledgement of John Mark as his son, Peter uses the word *uios*. This word is also used to describe the apostle John's relationship to Mary, the mother of Jesus. By contrast, Paul uses the word *teknon*, which normally means *child* and can be interpreted as male or female. The question arises as to whether Peter's description of Mark is thus more personal.

Peter likely used Mark as his writer for his letters. Mark then related Peter's recollection of events in the Gospel of Mark. Their acquaintance went back to the time of the crucifixion.

Paul knew Timothy and Titus in later years than Peter knew Mark. Paul was hesitant to use the word *uios* in describing his relationship with these spiritual children. However, it would certainly be pressing the issue of favoritism or closeness in either case. Thayer's *Greek-English Lexicon* offers a very thorough discussion of both words.[54]

SISTERS OF FAITH

The New Testament mentions women but not to the extent of the Old Testament. There is no Sarah, Rebecca, Rachel, Miriam, Deborah, Ruth, or Esther. Mary, the mother of Jesus, is mentioned throughout the Gospels but only briefly in Acts: "The apostles were all together. They were constantly praying with the same purpose. Some women, Mary the mother of Jesus, and his brothers were there with the apostles" (Acts 1:14 ERV).

During the ministry of Jesus, the name Mary was mentioned often. Martha and Mary of Bethany were given some biographical space. Mary of Magdala was also included as an avid follower of Jesus. Other women were mentioned as recipients of healing or compassion or both. When the church became a reality, what place would women occupy?

The first story about a woman in Acts is about Sapphira and her husband Ananias. Before this mention, there is a prelude of generosity:

> The whole group of believers was united in their thinking and in what they wanted. None of them said that the things they had were their own. Instead, they shared everything. With great power the apostles were making it known to everyone that the Lord Jesus was raised from death. And God blessed all the believers very much. None of them could say they needed anything. Everyone who owned fields or houses sold them. They brought the money they received and gave it to the apostles. Then everyone was given whatever they needed. (Acts 4:32–35 ERV)

The scriptures then explain that Ananias and Sapphira lied about the donation of property. In the story, the woman and the man were equal partners in their deceit, and both died because of it (Acts 5). As R. B. Rackham states, the couple was "individually provoking the Lord, trying how far the Spirit would abide and overlook the double heart; and cooperatively, testing the extent and reality of the Spirit's knowledge in the church."[55] The punishment of death seems severe, but the early group of believers saw the importance of being truthful to God. The contrast is made in Acts 4 with Barnabas who was a Levite born in Cyprus. He sold a field and gave the money to the apostles.

Peter had a very happy meeting when he went to the house of Mary, the mother of John Mark, after he was released from prison. Luke records that "many people were gathered there and were praying" (Acts 12:12 ERV). We can deduce that her home had become a church home for many in Jerusalem.

Her son, John Mark, had already become well known to the Christian community. He was to become a close companion of his relative Barnabas and accompanied him on mission ventures. Later, Mark becomes close to Peter and much later to Paul. Mary's leadership provided a needed place of security for the genesis of the church in Jerusalem. Rackham notes about Mary, "This introduces us to another Mary, another of those women whose praise was in the early church. The gate, i.e., the gateway into the courtyard and the maid or fortress, indicate the residence of a well-to-do-family. The house being spacious had become a kind of centre in the church."[56] Mary was the leader among the women and men in the stability of the church in Jerusalem.

More women of leadership were not apparent until Paul and his company left for Macedonia as recorded in Acts 16. "We left Troas in a ship and sailed to the island of Samothrace. The next day we sailed to the city of Neapolis. There we went to Philippi, a Roman Colony and the leading city in that part of Macedonia" (Acts 16:11–12 ERV). At Philippi they met a group of women at prayer at a river outside the city gates. At this place Paul and his companions Luke, Silas, and Timothy met a woman named Lydia. Rackham identifies the site as a prayer place or *proseucha* and the woman as Lydia: "She was really a native of Thyatira, a city of Lydia in the province of Asia and so she was called after her country Lydia."[57] Most Biblical scholars think that she was wealthy, being a merchant selling purple cloth.

The city of Philippi was a Roman colony, and Paul and his company were new on the continent of Europe. Asian and particularly Jewish customs were less known. Lydia thus became the first European to be exposed to and receptive of the gospel message. Paul had a vision while in Turkey or Asia Minor that Macedonians were waiting for a teacher. Since Paul was a Roman citizen, William Ramsay points out in his book that the opportunity was present as never before to reach Gentiles.

Lydia was, according to Ramsay, "a first-class dealer. She must have possessed a considerable amount of capital to trade in such articles."[58] He pointed out that Philippi bore the name of Philip II of Macedonia who was the father of Alexander the Great. It had become a Roman colony in 42 B.C. and home to a number of Roman soldiers. No synagogue was there since a quorum of ten male Jews was not present.

The river Gangites became the unofficial place of worship for several women who were God-fearers. "The leader of these women was Lydia, a God-fearer from the city of Thyatira in the province of Asia, who was an agent for the sale of purple dye, derived from the juice of the madder root, for which her native region was famed as early as Homer's Day. Since there was a Jewish colony in Thyatira, it was probably there that she had become a God-fearer." Such was the conclusion of F. F. Bruce in his book *Paul: Apostle of the Heart Set Free*.[59]

The story in Philippi became more complicated when Paul confronted a young woman who believed that she had certain supernatural powers. Ramsay concludes that she was a ventriloquist and not a witness to Christianity. He states:

> Her belief in her supernatural possession is certain; but it became thereby all the more acute in certain perceptions and intuition. With her sensitive nature, she became at once alive to the moral influence, which the intense faith by which the strangers were possessed gave them, and she must say what she felt without any definite idea of result therefrom. For the immediate utterance of her intuition was the secret of her power.[60]

Bruce comments that the young woman may have been possessed by some form of evil spirit, which he called "a pale imitation of the Pythian prophetess at Delphi, so that she became for the time being the mouthpiece of Apollo. The spirit that enabled the Philippian slave girl to tell fortunes was exorcised by Paul when she persisted in shouting unsolicited testimonials after him and his companions through the street of the city."[61]

Paul and his companion Silas were imprisoned because of the freeing of the evil spirit and the return of the young woman to normalcy. An earthquake released them from prison, and the jailer was converted to Christ as well as all those in his house. The story proceeded with the apology of the city officials to Paul and Silas when the officials found out that Paul and Silas were Roman citizens.

Luke recorded the final verses of Paul's stay in Philippi in this way: "But when Paul and Silas came out of the jail, they went to Lydia's house. They saw some of the believers there and encouraged them. Then they left" (Acts 16:40 ERV). Lydia thus became the first woman of significance to become a Christian in Greece and thus in Europe. She became the center of a church home. More than a successful businesswoman, she became a true Christian who extended great encouragement for the spread of the gospel to new frontiers. Bruce states, "Paul and Silas, with Timothy, moved on but by the time they did so they had gathered a promising young church together in Philippi. The last converts they made before leaving the place were the town jailer and his family."[62]

Paul met capable and caring women throughout his ministry. No misogyny is present in his writings. With Paul there was no distinction between Jew and Greek or male and female (Galatians 3:28). In Romans 16, Paul lists the names of men and women who had meant so much to him. Phoebe is one of those names, and she is called a leader or servant of the early church:

> I want you to know that you can trust our sister in Christ, Phoebe. She is a special servant of the church in Cenchrea. I ask you to accept her in the Lord. Accept her the way God's people should. Help her with anything she needs from you. She has helped me very much, and she has helped many others too. (Romans 16:1–2 ERV)

The sixteenth chapter of Romans demonstrates that women very early in church history became involved in the spread of the gospel message. Paul says of Persis: "She has also worked very hard for the Lord" (Romans 16:12 ERV). He also mentions "Tryphaena and Tryphosa, women who work very hard for the Lord" and the mother of Rufus, "who has been a mother to me too" (Romans 16:12–13 ERV).

Yet Phoebe seems to have a special place in the church at Cenchrea. Bruce states that Paul "treated women as persons: we recall his commendation of Phoebe, the deacon of the church in Cenchrea, who had shown herself a helper to him as to many others."[63] Phoebe is called a *diakonos* or servant. In many ways she was a special servant. As Bruce speculated, she may have delivered his letter to the Romans.[64]

Cenchrea in modern times lies under the water, and one can literally pick fragments of relics from the sea. Since it was a port of great importance, Phoebe could travel to Rome, and she displayed her great loyalty and courage in making the trip.

Hunter speculates that the church met in her home. "She also devoted her influence and means to the assistance of brothers landing at the port."[65] He also comments that the word *deaconess* would be too technical. "In the later church there was an order of deaconesses for special work among women owing to the peculiar circumstances of oriental life, but we have no reason to believe there was such an order at this early period."[66] Yet Phoebe demonstrated the assimilation of Godly women into the working fabric of the early church.

In the same chapter, Romans 16, Paul mentioned Priscilla, one of the most influential women of the early Christian community:

> Give my greetings to Priscilla and Aquila, who have worked together with me for Christ Jesus. They risked their own lives to save mine. I am thankful to them, and all the non-Jewish churches are thankful to them. Also, give greetings to the church that meets in their house. (Romans 16:3–5 ERV)

As previously noted, Paul met this extraordinary couple in Corinth:

> And he found a certain Jew named Aquila, a man of Pontus by race, lately come from Italy, with his wife Priscilla, because Claudius had commanded all the Jews to depart from Rome: and he came unto them; and because he was of the same trade, he abode with them, and they wrought, for by their trade they were tentmakers. (Acts 18:2–4 ASV).

Their connections with Paul were many. The part about the banishment in Corinth was preceded with some history of their persecution. As Ramsay notes:

Tiberias had deported 4,000 Roman Jews to Sardinia in the hope that the malaria might destroy them. And now about A.D. 49, Claudius had issued an edict banishing the Jews from the city altogether. Seutonius tells us of the reason; it was because the Jews were in a state of constant turmoil at the instigation of one Christus. These words no doubt refer to disturbances which ensued upon the preaching of the Christ at Rome similar to those in other Jewish Quarters, in Galatia and in Macedonia.[67]

Ramsay adds an interesting hypothesis: "Luke mentioned his Roman residence because it had some bearing on his subject. After some time (during most of which Paul had been in Aquila's company at Corinth and at Ephesus) a journey to Rome is announced as Paul's next intention. Aquila was able to tell him of the events that had occurred in Rome."[68] Thus, Paul's interest in the great city of Rome was increased by his contact with Aquila and Priscilla (Acts 18 and 19).

Bruce points out that this couple was engaged in the tentmaking business and "apparently were a 'well-to-do' couple. Their tent-making may have had branches in several centres with a manager in charge of the branches in those places where they themselves were not actually resident. They were thus able to move back and forth easily between Rome, Corinth, and Ephesus."[69]

Paul was able to form a lasting fellowship with this Christian family and to find a home where he could support himself if needed. Other than Barnabas and Silas, their friendship was an equality of knowledge and skill. In effect, Paul found a place of refuge and a lasting friendship among like-minded people who were more than ready to spread the gospel message. Bruce continues:

Now in Acts 18:2 the very harsh and strange arrangement of the sentence must strike every reader. But clearly the intention is to force on the reader's mind the fact that Aquila was a Jew while Priscilla was not, and it is characteristic of Luke to suggest by subtle arrangement of words a distinction which would need space to explain formally.[70]

Whatever their position, whenever the three Christians met, social and racial barriers were not present. They worked together to learn the scriptures and to teach the scriptures. The result was an example of Paul's remarks to the Galatian Christians that when in Christ, there is no Jew or Gentile or male or female, free person or slave (Galatians 3:26–28).

The adventures of Aquila and Priscilla continue in the scriptures. In writing to the Romans, Paul mentioned this couple again. They saved his life in Ephesus. As Rackham mentions:

Aquila illustrates the migratory character of much of the empire. It may have been at Rome that Aquila won his wife Prisca (or in the more diminutive form) Priscilla. Both names are Roman; and both have been found in the cemetery of the *Acilian Gens*, so that they may have been freedmen of that family. Because Priscilla's name is mentioned first, "she probably took the leading part in evangelistic work."[71]

Aquila and Priscilla moved as missionaries as recorded by Luke. In the city of Ephesus, they met the great orator Apollos whom they heard speaking in the synagogue. Acts 18:24–28 (KJV) describes Apollos as "an eloquent man, and mighty in the scriptures" who fervently and accurately taught the way of the Lord as he had been taught.

Apollos spoke boldly though he knew "only the baptism of John" (Acts 18:25 KJV). When Aquila and Priscilla heard Apollos preach, they intervened, taking him aside to teach him "the way of God more accurately" (Acts 18:26 ESV). Apollos's meeting with this Christian couple gives us insight into the cooperation of the early church. Although Apollos was by all appearances the greater scholar, he was willing to learn the more correct doctrine from dedicated followers such as Aquila and Priscilla.

Ramsay observes that Priscilla was mentioned in first order as a teacher:

> The unusual order, the wife before the husband, [Acts 18:18] must be accepted as original; for there is always a tendency among scribes to change the unusual into the usual. Paul twice mentions Prisca before Aquila. [2 Timothy 4:19 and Romans 16:3] Probably Prisca was of higher rank than her husband.[72]

Priscilla remained to the very end of Paul's life a helper and fellow Christian.

In Romans 16, he mentions Prisca or Priscilla in verse three. Denny, in *The Expositor's Greek Testament*, comments about the couple: "Paul met them first in Corinth. Here as in Acts XVIII, 26 and 2 Timothy IV,19, the wife is put first, probably as the more distinguished in Christian character and service."[73] Paul mentions that Aquila and Priscilla saved his life. Denny again concludes:

To save Paul's life Prisca and Aquila incurred some great danger themselves; what, we cannot tell. They were in his company both in Corinth and Ephesus, at times when he was in extreme peril. The language implies that the incident referred to had occurred long ago for all the Gentile churches to be aware of it, but yet, so recently that both they and the Apostle himself retained a lovely feeling of gratitude to his brave friends.[74]

Denny also mentioned that the church met in Aquila and Priscilla's home. The wording signifed "the body of believers meeting for worship there, a body which would only be part of the local Christian community."[75]

Christian women very early in church history became an integral part of church leadership. Just as Paul and Peter planned for the next generation of believers in the persons of Timothy and John Mark, the church quickly included women as church leaders. From Rome, Paul wrote to Timothy imploring the young minister to bring Mark to assist him (2 Timothy 4:11). In this letter he sent greetings from some fellow Roman Christians, among them a woman named Claudia, possibly one in whose home the church assembled (2 Timothy 4:21).

Other examples of house worship in the homes of women included Mary, the mother of John Mark; the home of Lydia; and the home of Phoebe. These women very likely suffered persecution as did the male believers. They also greatly encouraged the believers and non-believers as Peter described Tabitha, also called Dorcas, a woman "full of good works and acts of charity" (Acts 9:36 ESV).

CONCLUSION

The early church set the great example for believers of every generation. Reconciliation and openness to all people were the spiritual legacies for the next generation in the church's history. It remains the standard for the church today.

END NOTES

1. R. B. Rackham, *The Acts of the Apostles, an Exposition*, Metheun and Company, LTD London, 1957.

2. Ibid

3. *Thayer Greek English Lexicon of the New Testament*, Baker Book House Co., Grand Rapids, MI, 1987.

4. R. B. Rackham, *The Acts of the Apostles*

5. Ibid

6. Ibid

7. Ibid

8. Ibid

9. Ibid

10. F. F. Bruce, *The Acts of the Apostles*, The Tyndale Press, London, 1956.

11. Ibid

12. Ibid

13. R. B. Rackham, *The Acts of the Apostles, an Exposition*

14. F. F. Bruce, *The Acts of the Apostles*

15. R. B. Rackham, *The Acts of the Apostles, an Exposition*

16. *Biblica*, www.biblica.com/resources/scholar-notes/niv-study-bible/intro-to-mark/

17. *The Ecclesiastical History of Eusebius Pamphilus*, Book II, chapter 15

18. Burton Coffman, *Commentary on Mark*, Austin, TX, Firm Foundation Publishing House, 1975.

19. Ibid

20. Ibid

21. Ibid

22. Ibid

23. Earle McMillan, *The Gospel According to Mark*, Austin, TX, R. B. Sweet Co., 1973.

24. Ibid

25. Ibid

26. Ibid

27. F. F. Bruce, *The Acts of the Apostles*

28. Ibid

29. Ibid

30. Ibid

31. Ibid

32. S. F. Hunter, *International Standard Bible Encyclopedia*, Grand Rapids, MI, Wm. B. Eerdmans Pub. Co., 1960.

33. Ibid

34. F. F. Bruce, *The Acts of the Apostles*

35. A. S. Peake, *The Expositor's Greek Testament*, Colossians, Wm B. Eerdmans, Grand Rapids, MI, 1956.

36.   Marcus Dods, *The Expositor's Greek Testament*, Wm. B. Eerdmans, Grand Rapids, MI, 1956.

37.   R. B. Rackham, *The Acts of the Apostles, an Exposition*

38.   F. F. Bruce, *The Acts of the Apostles*, University Press, Aberdeen, 1956.

39.   Ibid

40.   R. B. Rackham, *The Acts of the Apostles, an Exposition*

41.   Ibid

42.   Ibid

43.   Ibid

44.   Ibid

45.   Ibid

46.   John Rutherford, *International Standard Bible Encyclopedia*, Eerdmans Pub. Co., Grand Rapids, MI, 1960.

47.   *Thayer's Greek-English Lexicon of the New Testament*, Baker Book House Co., Grand Rapids, MI, 1987.

48.   *The Ecclesiastical Church History of Eusebius Pamphilus*, Zondervan Pub. Co., Grand Rapids, MI, 1860.

49.   Ibid

50.   Ibid

51.   Ibid

52.   Ibid

53.   *Thayer's Greek-English Lexicon of the New Testament*, Baker Book House Co., Grand Rapids, MI, 1987.

54.   Ibid

55.   R. B. Rackham, *The Acts of the Apostles, an Exposition*

56.   Ibid

57.   Ibid

58.   William M. Ramsay, *St. Paul the Traveller and Roman Citizen*, G. P. Putnam's Sons, New York, 1904.

59.   F. F. Bruce, *Paul: Apostle of the Heart Set Free*, William B. Eerdmans, Grand Rapids, MI, 1984.

60.   William M. Ramsay, *St. Paul the Traveller and Roman Citizen*

61.   F. F. Bruce, *Paul: Apostle of the Heart Set Free*

62.   Ibid

63.   Ibid

64.   Ibid

65.   S. F. Hunter, *International Standard Bible Encyclopedia*, Wm. B. Eerdmans Pub. Co., Grand Rapids, MI, 1960.

66.   Ibid

67.   William M. Ramsay, St. Paul, the Traveller and Roman Citizen

68.   Ibid

69.   F. F. Bruce, *Paul: Apostle of the Heart Set Free,*

70.   Ibid

71.   R. B. Rackham, *The Acts of the Apostles, an Exposition*

72.   William M. Ramsay, *St. Paul, the Traveller and Roman Citizen*

73.   James Denny, *The Expositor's Greek New Testament*, Wm. B. Eerdmans Pub., Co., Grand Rapids, MI, 1958.

74.   Ibid

75.   Ibid

ABOUT THE AUTHOR

A native Tennessean, James Byers is a graduate of David Lipscomb College (now Lipscomb University) where he received a B.A. degree in Speech Communication and Biblical Studies; later he attended George Peabody College, completing requirements for certification to teach.

His life's career has revolved around service as a teacher in Williamson County Schools, as a minister in Tennessee, Georgia, Florida, and Hawaii, and with the Tennessee Department of Human Services for over 25 years. An avid reader and student of ancient and modern history, philosophy, archaeology, and the classics, he has combined that knowledge with intensive Biblical studies for adult Bible classes at Harpeth Hills Church of Christ. This book, as well as previous writings, grew out of studying for and teaching those classes.

As a member of the Mission Committee for 35 years, he developed a particular interest in the travels of Paul and his co-workers as they spread out across the then-known world preaching the gospel of Christ.

James and his wife Marie live in Nashville. Their son Tracy, his wife Eve Wade Byers, and their three children reside in Oklahoma.

ALSO
BY THE
AUTHOR

The Apostle John: A Blessed Life

Hope of Heaven: Expectations and Descriptions

Angels of Great Joy: God's Messengers of the Nativity

James, The Brother of Jesus

The Family of Jesus Christ

www.ingramcontent.com/pod-product-compliance
Lightning Source LLC
Chambersburg PA
CBHW060412050426
42449CB00009B/1959